For

Kathy
Lindsey
Barry

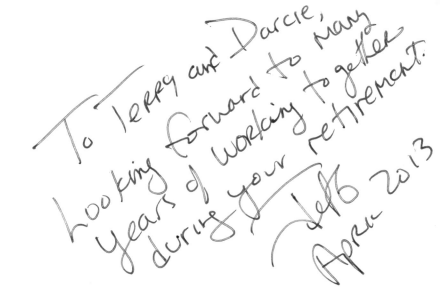

To Terry and Darcie,
Looking forward to Many
years of working together
during your retirement.

Jeff
April 2013

The Serious Money Train

Conversations About Managing
Your Money Seriously

Jeffrey David Ross , J.D. CFP®

ISBN: 061573880X

ISBN 13:   9780615738802

Acknowledgments

This book is all about Serious Money, encompassing more than thirty years of thinking and conversing about Serious Money. Along the way I've had two primary mentors. I want to properly and adequately acknowledge their respective contributions to my evolution and maturity as a financial advisor.

Nick Murray is the financial advisor's financial advisor. I first heard Nick speak in 1985. I've read most of his columns and books, and his advice monthly via his newsletter, *Nick Murray Interactive*. His is the constant voice of long-term optimism (to be understood as realism). Nick taught me to understand the value I provide as a financial advisor. He also taught me to understand and appreciate the value of Bear Markets, key principles and strategies for successful investing, and eight mistakes to avoid along the way. Last, but not least, Nick Murray taught me that investor behavior is the key determinant of long-term financial success. You will find these concepts (and more) interwoven liberally throughout this book.

Dan Sullivan is the entrepreneur's entrepreneur. Far and away, the most important decision I ever made as a financial advisor was to connect with Dan, co-founder of The Strategic Coach, a life-focusing program for entrepreneurs, in 1996. I've been attending Dan's workshops every 90 days since then; 16 years and counting. Dan taught me the value of setting goals, but more importantly, the process of reaching goals through better thinking. From Dan I learned that the problem isn't usually the problem —

the problem is not knowing how to think about the problem. Dan also taught me where rugged individualism should end and effective delegation should begin. He taught me the power of naming concepts and periodically focusing on my life path. You will find these concepts (and more) also interwoven liberally throughout this book.

Deanna Nowadnick assumes responsibility for managing the day-to-day client relationships and strategies at our firm, The Planner's Edge®, freeing me to engage our clients in important Serious Money Conversations.

Ayana Meissner assumes responsibility for managing our firm's day-to-day data flow, providing me with confidence that these Serious Money Conversations are based upon accurate information.

Mike Dubes was my brainstorming partner and story editor, coaching me through the doubts and anxieties of getting this book to print.

Table of Contents

Preface

A party of grad school friends at the University of Michigan in October 1980 produced the moment my career path began. A couple of drinks into the Halloween party, I excitedly bragged about growing my $2,000 IRA account into $2,400 just since springtime. My friends thought I was an investing genius when, in actuality, the stock market had simply lifted my boat with the rising tide of the 20% rally between Spring and Autumn 1980. We didn't know it at the time — and I'm glad we didn't — but we were falling prey to one of the oldest truisms in investing: "Never mistake wisdom for a bull market."

My friends saw only my investment success where they had none, and they became comfortable talking to me about their money and forays into the investment world. Then it happened for the first time: a friend asked, "I have $10,000; can you do the same thing with my money?" Another friend said, "I have $5,000; I'll let you invest it for me." By the time the night was over, five or six friends had offered to entrust me with their hard-earned money.

Of course, I had to say no because I wasn't a licensed investment advisor or broker. I had just graduated from The University of Michigan Law School and taken the Bar Exam, so I knew enough to refrain from giving investment advice without the proper credentials. But I enjoyed the feeling of being so trusted, and I wondered if I could earn a living helping others invest their money.

I recalled an experience two years earlier, after my graduation from law school, when I was confused and unsure about my future. My father had spent a small fortune for me to complete college and law school but I knew being an attorney wasn't (and never had been) in my heart. As the first college graduate in my family I felt a natural need to use my degree.

But it happened that Dr. Robert Schwitzgebel, a favorite professor from my college days, was giving a guest lecture at the university. He knew I lived in Ann Arbor, gave me a call, and we met in the living room of my apartment, replete with a $10 couch and a moving box that doubled as a coffee table.

As professors sometimes do, he offered advice that set me on the path that converged with the Halloween party conversations two years subsequent. He said to forget about the law degree as a credential, explaining that all the skills I had acquired during the three years of law school would never go unused. He asked a simple question: "What do you like to talk about?" My answer was immediate and equally simple: "Money." "There you go," he responded. And there I went, straight to The University of Michigan Law Library.

Since, at the age of 27, my investing experience consisted only of an Individual Retirement Account (IRA) with two no-load mutual funds, I naively researched the logistics of opening and managing one of these investment vehicles. But I quickly realized such an endeavor would distance me from what I liked to do, which was talking about money and investing.

Growing up in a family of entrepreneurs, I've always been comfortable talking about money. Dinner table conversations focused on the family businesses, treating customers well, saving money and investing wisely. I also learned two valuable lessons from my entrepreneurial family:

- Wealth can disappear quickly, as I witnessed my father losing his wealth quickly due to a few poor real estate deals.
- Wealth doesn't buy happiness or satisfaction, as I witnessed my uncle's substantial wealth become meaningless against the forces of alcohol and drugs.

I am also grateful that we were a golf-playing family. My stepfather used to preach that golf was a "character builder" because it teaches so many important life values. I've been able to rely upon those values and use them during my career. Golf teaches perseverance, integrity, a sense of fair play, sportsmanship and respect for others. Golf also teaches two skills important to financial success: staying calm in the face of adversity and being able to plan while staying in the present.

In the two years between my conversation with Dr. Schwitzgebel and my fortuitous Halloween party, I researched the 1974 breakthrough legislation known as ERISA, which was the new retirement law of the land. In fact, as I approached various banks in Ann Arbor about opening my first IRA account, I was surprised to learn that they knew virtually nothing about them. As a result, my first areas of expertise I developed on the way to becoming a financial advisor were retirement accounts and IRAs.

I became comfortable asking friends and colleagues challenging questions about their money and investing. I also learned about a new breed of financial advisor, known as financial planners. They work with clients face-to-face, evaluate their financial resources, learn about their dreams and aspirations, and help them figure out how to get from here to there during the course of their lives: a perfect fit for someone like me.

So I set about obtaining the necessary licensing credentials to become a practicing financial planner, including those from the securities industry and the College of Financial Planning. As one of the first Certified Financial Planners in the state of Washington, I mentored with a veteran planner, taught seminars on the subject and acquired a diverse and loyal clientele. We've spent over 30 years together, and it's been a privilege to help them identify their goals and then reach them, despite the vicissitudes of life that get in the way.

Many investment professionals have had long-lasting impacts on my thinking and development, and you will meet some of them and their pearls of wisdom throughout this book. There have been many significant events that became teachable moments because of their dramatic and unexpected entry into our lives — these too I will share with you. When

I made mistakes along the way, the lessons learned from them have proved to be much more important than the mistakes themselves. I will pass along these lessons to you as well.

I've learned that long-term financial success is not a matter of luck. It's also not a matter of picking the best investments or being in the right place at the right time. Long-term financial success is primarily a function of our own attitudes and behavior, a notion most investors never learn. My intent with this book is to provide the foundational tools, concepts and lessons that will allow you to create your own long-term financial success.

I wish you the best along your lifetime journey..

Jeffrey Ross, J.D., CFP®
Mercer Island, Washington
info@theplannersedge.com
www.theplannersedge.com
March 2013

Introduction

As an advisor to people with significant assets and complex financial lives, I am fascinated and motivated by helping them transform their complexities into simple game plans; game plans that create bigger and better futures, think through the important financial issues that inevitably present themselves, and achieve both their goals and long-term financial success.

Everyone takes a financial trip that lasts a lifetime, and I find it useful to think of the path to lifetime financial success as a great train ride. If we board in Los Angeles and New York is our destination, the route is never a straight line. It zigs and zags, and there are strange noises, dark tunnels and hair-raising curves as well. Uncertainty exists, and we will undoubtedly run into foul weather and delays that tempt us to change our destination or abandon our trip.

Investing, like travel, is part of our life experience. Arriving safely at our destination is the goal. The frustration, doubt and anxiety along the way can present significant obstacles, but they shouldn't prevent us from reaching our destination. Instead, they are the raw materials that help us recognize what is keeping us from our goal, and they identify what needs to be worked around and overcome with creative, strategic thinking.

If you've ever taken a long trip alone, you know how comforting it can be to have a traveling companion, particularly if that person is an experienced traveler. When unfamiliar or unexpected events occur during the trip, an experienced companion can provide reassurance that what may seem strange or frightening is merely the normal noise and vagary of travel. Successful investors likewise recognize the value of purchasing an extra ticket for a seasoned traveling companion, a financial advisor, a voice of reason that keeps us from overreacting and making a big mistake.

Given the obstacles certain to be in your way, how do you develop a reliable financial plan and a sound investment strategy that enables you to reach the New York of your life?

I'm writing this book for people who have accumulated significant assets and too much complexity during their financial journey. I want to be your knowledgeable traveling companion, to provide you with a Platform of Confidence so you can understand and implement a coherent approach to investing your Serious Money. I want to help you reach your destination with a minimum of stress and anxiety by providing strategic thinking and financial solutions that lead to long-term success.

My hope is that when you finish reading this book, you will have the confidence and peace of mind to be able to distinguish noise from wisdom, pursue a solid investment strategy, and choose a seasoned team that will care more about your money and success than anyone who doesn't share your last name.

I will offer a unique financial model that will introduce three principles to guide you through your journey. The model includes three investment strategies to help implement these principles.

Along our metaphorical trip, you will learn skills for handling situations that threaten the successful completion of your financial journey. You will learn to anticipate them, gain confidence, stay the course and ultimately reach your intended destination.

You will be able to enjoy the benefits that accrue from investing in the best businesses in the world, with an understanding and acceptance of the real risks. Equally important, you will learn how to avoid making the big mistakes that can permanently and irrecoverably damage your long-term lifestyle.

In short, you will become a more confident and relaxed long-term passenger on the great financial ride that is your life.

CHAPTER 1

Get on the Serious Money Train

(Three Ground Rules for a Platform of Confidence)

I work exclusively with Serious Money. I'm not interested in play money, speculative money, take-a-flyer money or who-gives-a-rip money. I care about the money you've earned, saved and invested for a dignified retirement or for your kids' and grandkids' college educations. I care about the money you've saved in your company's 401k or 403b plan during your working career, money that offers you one and only one chance to make the correct decision upon retirement. I care about the money you've inherited that you want protect and grow as a nest egg for your family and future generations, or the money you yearn to leave as a meaningful legacy to your favored charitable organization.

I believe everyone is on a long financial trip down their personal track that's like a train ride from Los Angeles to New York. But most people don't treat their money as Serious Money and they are not aboard the Serious Money Train. They are probably experiencing a pretty harrowing ride: holding tight to an outside railing and getting banged about as their train speeds along; or standing on the platform between cars, not sure which car they should enter; or flailing in the wind, like a cartoon character, holding onto the caboose by a finger.

You're reading this book because you treat your money as Serious Money. You have already accumulated a significant sum of your own Serious Money, or you are now ready to convert your heretofore non-Serious Money into Serious Money, and you want to develop the thinking and behaviors that grow and protect your Serious Money.

The Serious Money Train is for you. This is the Train that will get you from your Los Angeles starting point to your New York destination with guidance, discipline, intentionality, peace-of-mind and timely companionship. You will be comfortably seated in the passenger section enjoying the view, confident that you are on the correct track, with potential dangers under control and opportunities within reach.

Life is a Con Game–Set Goals

Confidence is important because life is a game of confidence. When you are feeling confident you can do most anything you set your mind to. When you are lacking confidence, you can't do much of anything. Take a moment for a quick inventory of your current financial confidence level:

- Do you feel confused, worried and stressed…or
  - Do you feel knowledgeable and confident with peace-of-mind?

- Are your accounts scattered and disorganized…or
  - Are your accounts organized and aligned?

- Are your investment risks maybe inappropriate...or
  - Are your investment risks definitely appropriate?

- Are you unsure about what you are doing...or
  - Are you are practicing sound investment habits and behaviors?

- Is the picture of your future faint or non-existent...or
  - Do you have a clear and powerful picture of your future?

- Are your expectations of your financial future low...or
  - Do you have a strategy for creating a bigger financial future?

- Are you unsure that you are on track...or
  - Do you know what track you are on?

- Are you trying to do it alone...or
  - Do you have a team of experts who care about you?

- Are you unprepared for unforeseen circumstances...or
  - Do you have contingency plans in place?

- Are you unclear whether you need or want help...or
  - Are you getting help from a trusted relationship?

It isn't difficult to improve your financial confidence. Many mistakenly believe that financial confidence is something you either have or you don't, perhaps something that occurs if you are lucky. Actually, confidence is the result of engaging in creative skills. Confident people create a goal and set a date when the goal should be achieved. Confident people paint vivid pictures of what life will look like when their goal is reached. They develop a checklist of every obstacle blocking their path to the goal, and figure out a strategy for handling each obstacle. The appearance of confidence stems from people behaving in alignment with their goals and knocking off the obstacles in their way, one by one.

This is Serious Money behavior. Although it might be new to you, it's a capability that is easily learned, and with practice, will help you experience confidence about the rest of your financial life. Since you're going to be on this great financial train ride for the remainder of your life anyway, why not develop the skills that will help you create your own Platform of Confidence?

Ground Rules for Your Platform of Confidence

Everyone's train ride involves investing, whether we like it or not. Saving your money is, of course, a good thing, but saving your money will take you only so far. With the rate of return on your savings being less than the increase in the cost of living, you cannot improve your lifestyle by simply saving money. It's unlikely you will even be able to *maintain* your lifestyle as the purchasing power of your savings erodes a bit each year.

Investing is the only route to enhance the purchasing power of your money, and it is probably the only route to maintain its purchasing power. Saving money is easy, which is one reason that it doesn't pay very well. Investing money isn't easy, which is why you need to develop a Platform of Confidence about investing in order to have a successful journey. Here are three basic ground rules of investing that will help construct your Platform of Confidence.

Ground Rule #1. It's Okay to Refresh Your Starting Point. Perhaps you are unhappy with your financial progress to date. Maybe you haven't made good decisions or feel you've been unlucky. You might have become unnecessarily frightened or grown fearful of the markets. You may think it's too late to do anything about the track you are on. But I'm suggesting that it's not too late to make a course correction. Wherever you are on your journey, you've already accumulated resources, experiences and lessons. Consider these to be your new starting point, an intermediate city along the route, as you now learn about a Serious Money approach for the rest of your journey.

Ground Rule #2. Don't Wait For a Better Time. Have you ever had money to invest but didn't think it was a good time? You waited for a better time but it never arrived, or the better time came but you didn't recognize it as a better time? These problems disappear when you follow the rule: *Buy when you have the money*. There is no better time to invest than when you have the money to invest. Often, though, people have objections to this ground rule. Let's address them:

- What if the market is falling or has just fallen, and the news media reports the outlook is bleak? How can that be a good time to invest? The answer is old as the hills: buy low and sell high. Prices are lower when things look bleak. You get more shares for the same number of dollars, and the next move after the decline ends is always up.

- What if the market has just risen? Shouldn't I wait for prices to drop back a bit? No, for two reasons: (1) you don't know when or if prices will come back to prior levels and (2) just because prices are higher than they were doesn't mean they won't go higher in the future than they are now.

- What if I just invested and the market drops? Was that still a good time to invest? Granted it would have been more opportune had you been lucky enough for the drop to occur before you had the money to invest, but it was still a good time to invest. Why? Because the likelihood of much higher prices in the distant future far outweighs the temporary downturn, and your time horizon is (or should be) long enough to sustain an initial drop for a short time in favor of bigger long-term increases.

<u>Ground Rule #3. Take Advantage of Big Sales.</u> Think Nordstrom sale. Just as you instinctively know to stock up on your seasonal clothes when Nordstrom is having their semi-annual sale, the same holds true when the stock market has a markdown of its prices. Your dollar will buy more shares when the price is lower.

The general tendency is to avoid buying when the stock market is falling, probably out of an irrational fear that the market won't stop falling, even though we know intellectually that in the past the market has always stopped falling and our dollar buys more shares at lower prices. We seem to feel more comfortable buying when the market is rising, prices are going up, and our dollars are buying fewer shares.

How to reverse this perverse psychology is going to be the subject matter of subsequent chapters. Until then, remember that market declines are like big sales at Nordstrom. You know what to do when that happens.

CHAPTER 2

Hang on to Your Manifesto

(The Three Serious Money Principles)

The Serious Money Train has a manifesto, a set of principles that guides your entire journey. Remember these Principles because they will be a source of strength and conviction when you are tempted to bail on your trip. The temptations are ever-present, as there always seems to be at least one economic problem causing worry and concern. I think of these as the *crisis du jour*. Some have thought that the budget deficit, high unemployment, China's growth, or European defaults appears to be a big enough problem to derail our economy. In the past, we've worried about inflation and hyperinflation, the runaway price of gold, the scarcity of oil, high interest rates and derivative trading, among others. Often, these worries recycle after they've been forgotten for a while.

The list goes on, from one crisis to the next, always trying to frighten you off the Train. The crisis du jour has an able accomplice: the news media. A lesson I learned many years ago is that the business of news is to sell news even if there isn't any news. We all know that the news media has a focus on the short term, and with competing 24/7 news cycles today, virtually all daily news is hyped beyond reasonable import.

Some stories are important, some events and trends significant, but most are just noise. If you can distinguish the noise from wisdom, you can summon the emotional fortitude to stay on the Train. Handling the noise is never easy, but understanding and relying upon the three Serious Money Principles will allow you to navigate the daily onslaught with knowing acceptance and calm.

Serious Money Principle 1: Faith in the Future

Faith in the Future is the foundational Serious Money Principle. It provides the reason for investing in the first place, the context for interpreting crisis stories, and the firewall you need to avoid making one of the Eight Big Mistakes.

In the Serious Money context, faith does not have a religious con-notation but rather recognition that the path of human progress moves inexorably upward. Despite all of the world's problems, the human race progresses towards greater freedom and knowledge, more inter-connect-edness between people and faster delivery.[1]

We rarely perceive the path of progress correctly, however, and if we do, it's not for very long. We tend to be overly positive or negative about the human condition. When optimistic, we tend to value the path very highly — until we over-value it enough for people to recognize that it can't be this good. When pessimistic, we place a low value on the path — until we under-value it enough for people to recognize that it can't be

---

1 For confirmation that we are on an upward path to solving the world's biggest problems, such as water, energy, health and education, read the breakthrough 2012 book by Peter Diamondis, *Abundance*.

this bad. We are in a constant cycle of optimism to pessimism and back again.

Picture the path of human progress as a straight yellow line, upwardly sloping, on a graph. Now picture a white line that oscillates over and under the yellow line, creating alternating peaks and troughs that correspond to the alternating perception cycle of optimism and pessimism. Let's relate this illustration to the stock market. Think of the yellow line as a rough approximation of the stock market, which is also upwardly-sloping when viewed from a long-term perspective. More accurately, the yellow line represents the path of the *true value* of the businesses in the stock market. The white oscillating line represents the path of our *collective perceptions* of the true value of these businesses, and our collective perceptions alternate between optimism and pessimism. This is why a graph of the stock market displays alternating peaks and troughs around a long-term average.

There is a common sense reason why the relationship between actual and perceived human progress so resembles the relationship between the actual value and the pricing of the stock market. The reason is that human progress creates economic development, which in turn makes things more valuable. Therefore, the world is continually becoming more valuable. The economic development is created by businesses and therefore businesses also become more valuable as they create value. But the true value of a share of a business is rarely perceived because investors are either too optimistic or too pessimistic about a business' future. Therefore, the price of a share of a business tends to fluctuate around its true value, just as the white line fluctuates around the yellow line.

Simply put, the reason to invest in the great businesses of the world is because the path of human progress is upwardly-sloping, making the world always more valuable. Since the value is primarily created by businesses, the businesses themselves become more valuable, and thereby increase in price. The trick is to recognize this Principle during the times when our collective pessimism makes it appear that the businesses of the stock market may soon be without value.

We see now why the Principle of Faith in the Future provides the underlying context and reason for being a long-term investor. But the Principle also provides a context for interpreting each new crisis that seems to pose an insoluble problem: you don't have to know how the problem is going to be solved; you can take solace in knowing that it will be solved, just as all the great problems in the past ended up being solved.

This Principle will also help you avoid making a mistake that could cause irrecoverable losses over your lifetime. There are Eight Big Mistakes (of which more will be written later) to avoid. Perhaps the most potentially damaging is Panic, which ensues when you have lost all faith in the future, when you have thrown Principle #1 under the bus. Panic causes you to sell out of fear that the crisis du jour will not only get worse, but that you will lose most or all of your money. When you panic out of the market you have only three choices remaining:

- Recognize your mistake *quickly*, reinvest at slightly higher prices, minimizing your lost opportunity from the next market recovery;

- Recognize your mistake *slowly*, reinvest at much higher prices, maximizing your lost opportunity from the next market recovery, and;

- Fail to recognize your mistake, never again invest in the market, converting the temporary loss in value of your investment into a permanent, irrecoverable loss.

Do you remember where you were on Black Monday, October 19, 1987? This was the day that the stock market (i.e., the Dow Jones Industrials Average) fell 508 points, the largest single day decline (percentage-wise, almost 23%) in market history. I remember the panic, news reports of brokers committing suicide and the widespread sense of a complete loss of faith.

But I also remember the impact of two wise investors who taught me in real time how important it is not to panic. On that Monday evening, I watched the legendary Sir John Templeton, storied investor and founder of the Templeton family of mutual funds, on television. He calmly and objectively recited 4 or 5 feats of human progress that had been or were about to be achieved, and explained that they were just being temporarily hidden from view. There was no need to panic, the world was not coming to an end.

The very next day I attended a luncheon meeting with John Rogers, the manager of the Ariel Growth Fund. He discarded the speech he had intended to give, and spoke from the heart about the losses his fund had suffered the day before, his fears about what was ahead and his confusion as to how to respond. He also shared what he chose to do the previous evening in his hotel room: he re-read the 1841 classic, *Extraordinary Popular Delusions and the Madness of Crowds*, in particular the chapter on the Dutch tulip mania in the 1700's. He awoke the morning of the luncheon with a calm attitude that the previous day's mania too shall pass.

Sir John Templeton and John Rogers taught me one of the most important lessons of my career: It's okay to be scared, but it's not okay to act on the fear. This is sage advice from two very smart guys.

Serious Money Principle 2: Patience

Serious Money Principle 1 speaks to the "how" of our insoluble problems; Serious Money Principle 2 speaks to the "when" of the solution. Principle 1 frees us of having to know *how* the problem will be solved before we allow ourselves to stay on the Train, and Principle 2 frees us of having to know *when* the problem will be solved before we allow ourselves to stay on the Train.

In both instances, it's enough to know that the problems will be solved. Knowing when won't actually help you become a better investor or help you achieve long-term success because an actual solution or even the certainty of a solution is not necessary for a market recovery. Often, just a hint that the crisis has turned the corner and is moving in the right direction will rally the markets significantly. If you wait until you think the solution is in place, you will be too late to prosper from the solution.

Additionally, the market is never focused solely on one problem and one solution. I don't think you can ever be sure what factors are influencing the market at any given time, despite the 10-second rationalizations offered by news pundits about the market's behavior each day. There are too many factors in play across the board. The market is a reflection of the simultaneous collective opinions, fears, hopes and strategies of millions of investors.

While it's true every investor is trying to make more money, some are trying to make more money that day, some over the short-term, some over the long-term and some over the very long-term. Some investors hope to make money by having prices drop while most hope to make money from a rising market. Investors bring their own circumstances, timing and opinions to the market. Waiting for a fix to a particular problem before beginning or resuming an investment just doesn't make sense, given the complexity of the system you are trying to out-guess.

One thing we know about patience within the context of investing is that it is indeed a virtue. A lesson I learned years ago is that the odds favor investors with longer-term perspectives. Here is an example: there are 85 years in the period from 1926 through 2011. The market performed positively in 72% of the years and negatively in 28% of the years, indicating that a winning market occurs most years, but there is still about a 1 in 4 chance of losing money in any given year.

Let's take a longer-term perspective and see if our odds improve. There are 77 ten-year time frames during the same 1926-2011 period. There have been only 5 ten-year periods that delivered negative returns (2010 being the most recent), whereas there have been 72 ten-year periods that have delivered positive returns. The ten-year perspective yields a 93% "success" rate whereas the one-year perspective's success rate is only 72%. This illustrates why Patience is one of the Serious Money Principles.

If you think of investing as a race between the tortoise and the hare, history shows that the hare typically ends up as road kill and "slow and steady wins the race." This is an important corollary to the Patience Principle, adding to your confidence about successfully reaching your destination.

I learned the importance of slow and steady the hard way, but once learned, it's become a valuable arrow in my investing quiver. It was during the go-go 1990's that I gave up on a world-class slow and steady manager in favor of a very popular hare. Jean-Marie Eveillard was the legendary manager of SoGen International (renamed First Eagle Global). His brilliance was evident not only by his 15%+ annual compounded return from 1979 through 1997 but also by the steadiness of his returns, never falling more than 20% top-to-bottom during any down period. However, Eveillard's steady style, returning "only" 5% per year for 1998-1999, suffered against the scorching 60%+ returns being turned in by managers of high tech and dot.com funds.

Eveillard's fund lost over 40% of its asset base, not because the fund decreased in value, but rather because advisors like me pulled our clients' money from the fund to invest in the high-flying hares. What did Jean-Marie do? Did he change his style to capture some of the dot.com magic or did he maintain the patient perspective he had always exhibited, waiting for returns to come his way again? In fact, he held his ground, stuck to his knitting, watched the dot.com bubble expand and then burst, and was able to shake his head at the hares that lay alongside the road. During the three years of 2000-2002, the NASDAQ Composite declined a compounded average of 30% per year whereas Jean-Marie's fund gained a compounded average of 11% per year.

Are you wondering whether it was better to be the hare, up an average of 60% for two years and then down an average of 30% for three years, or the tortoise, up an average of 5% for two years and then up an average of 11% for three years? Well, for the 5 year period, 1998-2002, the NASDAQ Composite's total net return was -14.95% and Eveillard's SoGen International fund was +47.47%. What this means is the high-flying hares turned a $100,000 investment into $85,050 but Eveillard turned $100,000 into $147,470 during the same period.

The moral of the story: slow and steady wins the race.

Serious Money Principle 3: Discipline

If you can accept that you don't know how the world's problems are going to be solved and that you don't know when they will be solved, then you will be less likely to have the problem with Serious Money Principle 3, Discipline, that other investors do.

Principle 3 suggests it is better to do things that have always worked than try things that have almost never worked. Pity the investor who tries to outguess the market and figure out how things will get worked out, or who tries to time entries and exits based on guesses. He's willing to try almost any new-fangled investment instrument, strategy or "expert". The investor who plans for the long haul and has faith that problems get solved in their own time is quite satisfied to use tried-and-true strategies, investment instruments that have proven their worth over time and seasoned experts who follow time-honored approaches.

Can any aphorism be truer than "buy low, sell high"? Can an investment concept be any simpler? Why is it so hard to put into practice? The answer is discipline, or more accurately, lack of discipline.

When the market is going up and up, investors tend to believe it will continue to go up forever, so they buy more shares at higher prices to avoid missing out on such a bonanza. Of course, the market has never gone up forever, so it's undisciplined to believe it will this time. When the market is plunging, investors tend to believe it will continue to go down forever, so they sell at lower prices to avoid losing all their money. Except that the market has never gone down forever, so it's also quite undisciplined to believe it will this time. This pattern of undisciplined investing turns "buy low, sell high" upside down, and it's easy to see how it happens, isn't it?

The financial industry is continually developing new products to sell to investors. These begin with good intentions, but typically try to capture a segment of the market that has already risen in price. Sometimes they attempt to solve a problem investors didn't even know was a problem until they were sold the solution. Without a set of principles to follow, investors can fall prey to the newest and hottest investment ideas with a crash-and-burn ratio that may demolish years of investment progress. We don't have to stretch our memories very hard to recall derivatives, CMO's, limited partnerships, and sub-prime mortgages.

You can enjoy a long, successful Serious Money Train Ride using just the basics: stocks, bonds and mutual funds. These investment instruments work.

A strategy that has always worked over the long run is buy-and-hold. It's boring, seems too easy and will probably be demeaned by your more sophisticated friends. But it works! It's always maligned when the market turns down ("Why would you hold with the market going down?"), but the strategy struts its stuff when the market abruptly turns up because you will be fully invested when it does. Market timers who feel smug about getting out of the market in time to avoid most of a downturn still face a dilemma: do they jump back in now after missing the first 20% of the upturn or do they wait for a pullback that may or may not happen? What a relief it is to be in the buy-and-holder's shoes at that moment.

Chuck Royce is known as the guru of small company investing. I met him in 1983 and I remember sitting in my Bellevue, Washington office with Chuck as I quizzed him about the different investments I was learning and recommending to clients. Chuck, who had at least 20 more years of experience than I had at that time, stated that he couldn't help me with the other stuff because he knew only about one thing: small companies. That's all he knew and all he did. He had no regrets about being a specialist, sticking to what he understood and avoiding anything he didn't understand.

Although I learned this lesson a bit later than I wished (since I had already recommended a number of investments to clients that I didn't fully understand and that never performed as hoped for), I am grateful for having learned it as early in my career as I did.

Sticking to what you know and understand is another sign of being a disciplined investor. In addition to being a bit boring, being disciplined in this way often results in counterintuitive and contrarian behavior that is different from that of your friends and colleagues. Learn to feel good about this as it is probably a sign that you are on the correct track.

In summary, the Serious Money Train's manifesto has three Principles designed to keep you on the Train, even when every fiber of your being is yelling for you to get off:

- Have Faith in the Future, even though you don't know how the problems are going to be solved;

- Have Patience, even though you don't know when the problems are going to be solved; and

- Have the Discipline to do what has always worked.

CHAPTER 3

Stay on the Train

(Three Key Strategies)

Now that you are on the Train with Serious Money Principles to guide and protect you, it's time to discuss three strategies that will help ensure the success of your journey. The first strategy divides your money into two pools serving different purposes; the second spreads your money so all of your eggs aren't in one basket; the third protects your profits by taking advantage of higher prices.

Before we discuss the strategies, however, be sure to separate your "pillow" money from your investment money. Pillow money is your emergency cash. The recommended amount is typically equivalent to three months of normal monthly expenses. This amount may work for you but I think a better rule of thumb is to set aside whatever amount allows you to rest comfortably on the pillow at night without losing sleep.

Strategy 1: Two Pools of Money

After funding your pillow account with emergency cash, the rest of your money is available for investment strategies. Create two pools with this investment money: a *Lifestyle Pool* and a *Profit-Making Pool*. As I explain this strategy, you will see how the two pools interact to create a perpetual cycle of protecting and growing your investment money.

The Serious Money Lifestyle Pool protects your money by investing in fully liquid cash equivalents or short-term bond funds. You access this pool for cash to fund lifestyle needs that arise, such as a new car, big family trip, major home repair or business opportunity. If you are retired and dependent on cash flow from your investment money to supplement other sources of income, the Lifestyle Pool will send you monthly checks.

Don't try to be a hero with the Lifestyle Pool. You're not trying for the highest rate of return with this money. It's your safe money, accessible within 24 hours with virtually no risk of loss. Your goal for the money in this pool should be preservation so search for and accept the going rate of return.

Big Mistake Alert! You may be enticed to try to do just a bit better than the going rate when you see advertisements or recommendations for an investment that can "safely" double or triple the going rate. Don't do it! *Stretching for yield*, one of the Eight Big Mistakes, means ignoring an investment's potential total return to receive a higher interest rate. The reason it's a mistake is that a higher-than-competitive interest rate means the borrower (the company or government entity) is deemed to be a bit riskier. This means there is a greater chance that the borrower will become unable to continue paying the higher rate or even default on repayment of the borrowed money.

Total return is composed of interest plus or minus the change in share price. Let's say Investment A's interest yield is at the going rate of 2% and the price stays steady. Its total return therefore is 2%. If Investment B's interest is triple the going rate at 6% but its price erodes by 10% due to the perceived or actual risk of losing principal, its total return is minus 4% (the 6% interest minus the 10% loss of principal). Don't stretch for yield at the risk of losing principal. Remember, this is your safe money. You will have upcoming needs so you can't afford to lose it.

You will be using this money and depleting the Lifestyle Pool over time. You will need a source of money that can replenish the depleted amounts. That source is your second pool of money, the Serious Money Profit-Making Pool. This is your pool of money that is invested for growth of principal. It will be at risk in order to produce rewards. When this pool earns a pre-determined level of profits, you will harvest some or all of the profits and send them to the Lifestyle Pool, thereby replenishing any monies you've already depleted. This allows you to continue to withdraw money for future cash needs.

The money in the Profit-Making Pool should be invested in quality equity positions. Equity investments are necessary because fixed income investments won't provide enough real growth over time. Only equity investments have the potential to grow the average 8-10% per year you need to maintain and enhance the purchasing power of your Lifestyle Pool.

Because this Pool is for growing profits you do not need to dilute your returns by balancing your equities with other asset classes, such as cash, fixed income, precious metals or real estate. If you adequately fund your Lifestyle Pool in the beginning you will be able to withstand a prolonged Bear Market in your Profit-Making Pool without being tempted off the Train or forced off the Train for lack of cash.

But isn't investing 100% of your Profit-Making Pool into the stock market a big gamble? Isn't the stock market just a big casino?

The answer is no. The stock market is not like a casino. In a casino, if you play long enough the house will win because the odds are in the house's favor. In the stock market, if you play long enough you will win because the odds are in your favor. The key is to invest for the long-term, which you can now do because you have sufficient cash in your Lifestyle Pool.

Big Mistake Alert! Just because you have sufficient cash in your Lifestyle Pool doesn't mean you should speculate with the equities in your Profit-Making Pool. *Speculation* is another of the Eight Big Mistakes. This is where you choose investments for their price change instead of their potential increase in underlying value. Examples are gold, oil and commodities, where the only thing that can happen is price change — it either goes up or down. These price movements are largely out of your control and place your Profit-Making Pool at risk of losing significant chunks of its value, thereby also placing your Lifestyle Pool at risk of not being replenished soon enough to meet your cash needs in the future.

How much should be in your Lifestyle Pool? You should fund an amount sufficient to carry you through the next Bear Market in your Profit-Making Pool, plus a little more in case you under-estimate its length. In other words, you need an amount that will fund your cash needs when there isn't any replenishment money from the Profit-Making Pool until the next Bull Market begins anew.

Strategy 2: Funds That Make Sense

The best investment vehicle for your Profit-Making Pool's equity money is the time-tested mutual fund. You should screen for funds that are internally diversified across hundreds of great businesses and managed by world-class managers who walk the walk. A Serious Money Manager has a minimum of 20 years of experience and a proven track record. Five or six great funds are enough to sufficiently diversify your portfolio, provide liquidity and grow your pool during Bull Market advances.

Not all equity mutual funds are created equal. Each has a manager who operates within a pre-defined discipline, style or approach aimed at making money in the stock market, and there are as many ways to approach making money in the market as there are managers.

Managers also differ in their sense of responsibility about making money for you. Some manage your Serious Money seriously and others do not. You might assume that all managers would treat your money seriously, but I've found this not to be true over my 30+ years of mutual fund investing. Some managers stay fully invested regardless of market and pricing conditions. They reason that if you give them money, you are willing to assume the attendant risks, and that you will take your money away when you are no longer willing to assume the risks. In other words, their job is to invest your money the way they said they would, and the results will either be successful or not.

Other managers think differently. They believe they should treat the money you give them as though it was their own. They invest in businesses when they think the odds are good that those businesses will increase in value. They sell when the value has been realized, and they are willing to hold cash until the price of the businesses they want to buy are at an opportune level. These are Serious Money Managers.

The Serious Money Managers I recommend to our clients are "value investors", managers who believe the best way to make a good return is to buy at the right price. In fact, buying at a low price is mandatory. They also believe that the time to sell their shares in a business is when the price of the shares has reached a fully-priced level. They don't try to squeeze every last drop of juice out of the orange because they don't want to risk holding the bag if and when the price begins to retreat from over-priced levels.

Serious Money Managers tend to eat their own cooking; that is, they and their employees invest their own money in the fund. They gain when you gain and they suffer when you suffer. You share a commonality of interest with the manager. This is a recipe for successful results.

What is the correct way to spread your money around to the various managers? I recommend picking five or six quality managers who:

- Have an approach that you understand;
- Walk their talk;

- Eat their own cooking;
- Own up to their unsuccessful picks, and
- Stick to their knitting even when their approach is temporarily out of favor.

The last item in this list is not as easy as it might sound because many good managers give up on their style when the winds are blowing at the back of a different style. I learned this lesson in the nineties when a top-ranked manager, who had made his reputation investing in well-known growth companies like Colgate-Palmolive and Coca-Cola, suddenly decided to begin investing in high tech and dot.com companies when those returns started becoming spectacular. Unfortunately, his switch in style came too late and his fund suffered 50%+ losses, giving back years of hard-earned profits. If instead he had ridden out the bursting of the tech bubble in 2000 with his old-style businesses in the portfolio, the fund would have had a very modest loss, easily recoverable.

I believe that successful investing is an art, not a science. As such, the best we can hope to find is a handful of disciplined managers who walk their respective talks. Doing this, you will automatically end up with adequate diversification across various styles. Your portfolio will own an assortment of large and small companies, domestic and foreign companies, value and growth companies.

The notion of investing as art is not conventional wisdom. Most advisors treat investing more scientifically by first determining the percentage you should have in each of the style boxes and then finding managers who say they will invest (and not deviate) from their respective styles. This approach can be successful but I believe it places too much faith in pre-defined percentage allocations and not enough faith in the ability of a good manager to make money outside the rigid constraints of a style box.

Index funds and ETFs are another approach to building an equity portfolio, although it is not the favored approach for your Serious Money. These vehicles hold a fixed basket of stocks within a specified sector of the market, and you can expect the basket's performance to equal the return of the individual stocks within the basket, minus a small management fee. Typically, the lower management fee is the main attraction of index funds and ETFs, but I do not believe the cost savings justify the loss of a skilled active manager who decides what to buy, what to sell, and when to buy and sell.

Big Mistake Alert! While five or six world-class fund managers is sufficient to achieve a balanced and diversified portfolio, many investors conclude that more is better and so they stake positions in 10-15 funds. I consider this one of the Eight Big Mistakes for two reasons: (1) with 10% or less in each position it is difficult to realize significant profits should one or two of the positions have strong performance; and (2) the quantity of funds becomes a substitute for having a coherent philosophy or strategy.

Big Mistake Alert! On the other hand, it's also one of the Eight Big Mistakes to load up on essentially one big theme.

There are many ways to make this mistake. For example, I've seen company employees who earn substantial salaries and also invest heavily in shares of their company's 401k and Employee Stock Option Plans. There is a natural incentive to load up on company shares because of the purchase discount. A serious situation can develop, however, if the company runs into a headwind: not only will the client's asset base erode quickly and disproportionately, but the client's income stream could also be in jeopardy.

Another common mistake is false diversification. This phenomenon struck hard during the tech bubble heyday of the late 1990s, when nearly every fund manager bought businesses they expected to benefit from the emerging digital economy. These funds were buying the same businesses or trying to benefit from the same idea. This left investors, who may have owned 5-10 different funds, believing they were diversified when they were really exposed to the same single new economy theme. The result was a "diversified" portfolio that fell apart when the new economy theme blew up beginning March 2000.

Strategy 3: Protect Your Profits

The primary goal of the Serious Money Profit-Making Pool is to grow profits, but the secondary goal is to protect those profits so they can be deposited into your Lifestyle Pool, either to replenish depleted cash flow or to save for future cash flow needs. Taking profits at the appropriate time means you will always be selling your shares "higher," which is one half the time-tested maxim "buy low, sell high."

Some investors attempt to protect their profits with a strategy of market timing. They follow the technical price patterns of the market to try to predict a low point for purchasing their shares, and they try to predict when the market will be at a high point to sell their shares. The advantage of this strategy is that it's simple to understand: just buy low and sell high. But one problem with this strategy is that it is impossible to consistently predict when the market is low and when it is high. After all, the strategy attempts to predict the net result of all the behaviors of all the investors everywhere even though it is virtually impossible to predict tomorrow's weather consistently.

An even bigger problem with market timing is the need to be correct all of the time. One bad call can ignite a series of problems down the line. Suppose you correctly predict that the market is about to begin to tumble so you sell all of your shares at a high point. For the time being, you feel very good about your decision because the price of your shares does indeed start declining and you have your cash in hand. This is all well and good, but to avoid being out of your shares forever you have to decide when to buy back.

If you buy back too early before prices have bottomed, you will be able to buy more shares than you originally had because the price is lower, but you may still see your shares continue to tumble.

If the price bottoms out and begins to climb upwards, your decision becomes difficult because you don't know if the climb is temporary or permanent. If you conclude the climb is temporary you will wait for the price to come back. But what if it doesn't? You are now left behind, having missed a great buying opportunity at lower prices. The more the shares climb in price, the more reluctant you become to buy because you missed the bottom and want another crack at it. Two things may happen now: (1) you may never be able to buy back low or (2) you eventually buy back at higher prices, resulting in the same or fewer shares than you originally had when you first sold. After you buy back at higher prices, the shares could fall back again, whipsawing your strategy into more losses.

And this scenario entails only one round trip of selling and rebuying. The market timer is doomed to try to make correct round-trip decisions repeatedly. Day traders and masochists may enjoy this Sisyphusian task, but it is not a good strategy for the Serious Money Investor. A better strategy is to instead set price targets based on your specific cash flow needs. Our business dubbed this *The Serious Money Target Strategy*. With this strategy, you do not have to predict when prices are going to be higher; you just have to monitor when the value of your portfolio has reached a pre-determined target level, and then execute the target.

Here's a simple illustration. Let's say you want to buy a $50,000 car. Go ahead and establish a target value for your portfolio that is $50,000 higher than today. When the portfolio gains $50,000 in profits, simply harvest the profits from your positions. By definition, you will have sold at higher prices and you don't have to predict whether the market is at a high point or when to rebuy.

Setting targets like this works for replenishing your Lifestyle Pool as well. Let's say you have $120,000 in your Lifestyle Pool generating $5,000 checks each month to supplement your other revenue sources. Your Lifestyle Pool will be depleted in two years. Let's assume also that your Profit-Making Pool has $1.2 million dollars invested in equity mutual funds. Here are two (of many) ways you could establish a profit-harvesting Serious Money Target system:

- Monitor your portfolio so that when it grows by $120,000 (a 10% up move) you harvest 100% of these profits and replenish your Lifestyle Pool;
- Decide instead to let your portfolio grow by $240,000 (a 20% up move) then harvest 50% of the profits, thereby replenishing your Lifestyle Pool with the harvested $120,000 and leaving $120,000 in the portfolio to continue to grow and compound.

There is no market-predicting or decision-making involved. You just need the discipline to execute your target when the target is reached. This strategy is simple to understand and effective. It has the important benefit of never requiring you to sell your shares at a low price to accommodate a need for cash. The strategy even works in a sideways market because there are always market rallies inside of the normal oscillations of a sideways market.

Our firm developed this strategy in 2001 after we watched our clients' portfolios grow significant profits during the 1990's, only to see those profits evaporate when the bubble burst in 2000. We needed to develop a better strategy for protecting profits after they had been earned. We've now successfully managed this strategy for our clients for over a decade, navigating through the up market of 2002-2008, the down market of 2008-09, and the rebound market of 2009 through 2012.

In summary, you can successfully ride the Serious Money Train if you adhere to and honor our three Serious Money Principles through thick and thin, and follow these three strategies:

- Separate your money into two pools, a Lifestyle Pool and a Profit-Making Pool;
- Build a 100% equity portfolio inside the Profit-Making Pool, utilizing 5-6 world-class mutual fund managers who have approaches that you fully understand; and
- Protect your profits by setting portfolio targets and having the discipline to harvest the profits when your targets have been reached.

CHAPTER 4

Severe Fog Ahead

(Three Fundamental Conditions)

You now have the three underlying principles and three behavioral strategies you need to jump on and enjoy the Serious Money Train Ride. However, you will be tested repeatedly along the route. There will be temptations to exit the Train and sabotage the entire ride. You will be subjected to countless moments where your personal investor behavior will be the difference between success and failure. The intent of the remaining chapters is to help you pass these tests with confidence.

One such test will be what I call The Financial Fog. The Fog isn't so much a solitary event as it is part and parcel of daily life. It's created by certain *fundamental conditions* of today's world combined with *distracting messages* from the media in response to these conditions. The resulting Fog affects three key areas of vulnerability in your life: your future, your assets and your family.

Fundamental Condition 1: Your Life is Busy

We live in an increasingly fast-paced and busy world. You go about your daily life, fulfilling existing commitments, obligations and expectations, invariably adding new ones but rarely deleting any. Each adds another layer of complexity in your life: when you open another new account; when you forge another new relationship that creates new responsibilities; or when you install another new technology that ratchets up the pace of everything else. Common sense tells you to slow down, think about things, and be careful about adding more personal complexity to your life.

Meanwhile, the omnipresent media clamors for your attention with messages that are about moments and short-term urgencies. The newest gadget should be bought to be in the know; the hot stock should be bought to avoid missing out; the latest problem should be viewed as a crisis to increase worry. Rarely does the media report anything within the context of a long-term perspective, but that's exactly what you know you need and what you are trying to achieve on your long Train Ride. Combine a busy world with the short-term perspective of an intrusive media, and your ability to create a clear and powerful picture of your future may be fogged. This leaves you vulnerable to a host of unintended outcomes.

The Serious Money Approach recommends two behaviors that will combat this lethal combination of conditions: first, develop a plan; second, visit it regularly.

The plan we develop with our clients is called a *Serious Money Vision Map*. It's created via a series of important conversations that evolve from a single, important question: "Picturing yourself in the future, looking back to the present, what has to happen for you to feel happy with your progress?" Your future reference point for this question can be 1, 5, 10 or even 25 years out.

Consider any particular dangers you need to avoid or eliminate, typically those that involve losing something valuable. List these dangers. Next, think about any particular opportunities you want to capture or attain, generally those that involve gaining something valuable. List these opportunities. Finally, think about the strengths you want to optimize, which generally involve your resources and relationships. List these strengths.

Now list all your financial accounts: bank, brokerage, mutual fund, life insurance, retirement, employer pensions, real estate parcels, debt obligations and the like. Think about when and why you opened these accounts, what's worked and what hasn't, and whether they are still important to you.

Next, list your current spending patterns for housing, medical expenses and your overall lifestyle. Which expenses have a termination date (e.g., a car loan or mortgage)? What new future expenses do you anticipate?

Your lists of current resources and spending, what's worked and what hasn't, along with your dangers, opportunities and strengths represent your current Family Story.

The next step in the process of creating your plan is transforming your Family Story into a clear, powerful picture of your financial future. This involves projecting each of your resources and spending obligations into the future, given expected rates of return and inflation factors.

The resulting picture will tell you what track you are on and whether you should feel satisfied with your progress. It will also help you identify any obstacles in your path. Once identified, you will be able to develop strategies for dealing with these obstacles. When you think about it, obstacles are your friends. They become the raw material needed to reach your goals.

I acknowledge that your plan is easier to describe than to develop. If you are not confident of your proficiency projecting numbers into the future, ask a trusted financial advisor to help you. Remember to review your plan periodically, preferably every 90 days. A quarterly review is ideal: it's a long enough period for lots of life to happen but short enough to clean up any messes before they become overwhelming.

If you invest the time and effort to create a clear, powerful picture of your future and develop the discipline to review your plan every 90 days, you will be doing something rare in our society, something that adds to the certainty of a successful ride down your financial path.

Fundamental Condition 2: Your Life is Risky

We live in a world full of risk. Your assets may be exposed to *undue or unknown risk at many* levels, including global (e.g., war), governmental (e.g., new taxes) and family (e.g., adult kids returning home). There are risks related to money: inflation, interest rates, business failure and leverage. Perhaps the most worrisome risk is the loss of your money. Common sense tells you to find the best ways to protect your money.

Meanwhile, there is rarely any risk message from the media, which instead seems to be about picking big winners and top performers. Virtually every financial magazine and website has its own "Ten Best" list: smart money tips, untapped money-making investment ideas or stocks to buy now.

When a risky world combines with a media focused on winners, your ability to distinguish important risk from irrelevant risk may be fogged, leaving your assets vulnerable to dramatic shrinkage. The Serious Money Approach requires a proper perspective of real risk to effectively combat this destructive combination.

The risk that Serious Money Investors must understand and appreciate above all is this: purchasing power risk. This is the risk that your money won't be able to buy as much lifestyle in the future as it can now buy. It's the most prevalent risk you encounter along your financial Train Ride because your cost of living is always increasing, and your money must have the ability to keep up. If not, you will fall behind and your future lifestyle will suffer commensurately.

There is a right and wrong way to protect against this risk. I learned about the latter in a personal way by watching how my grandmother Evie lived the last 45 years of her life. She was widowed in 1959 at the age of 45, inheriting a substantial nest egg of $200,000. She used this money to buy bank CDs and US Treasury notes for 45 years until she passed away at age 90 in 2004. She used the interest from these fixed income instruments to first supplement her salary and then her pension and social security.

Throughout the high-interest rate years of the 1970's and into the 1980's, Grandma Evie lived comfortably because her $200,000 account generated $20-30,000 annually. I was the oldest grandchild of 8, and we would all receive wonderful gifts for our birthdays and Hanukkah, along with her traditional stick of gum tucked inside a card. But when interest rates began to decline precipitously during the late 1980's and early 1990's, the extra income from her accounts plunged to $2-3,000 per year. No longer were there Hanukkah gifts for the grandchildren, just birthday gifts. And the birthday gifts were just the stick of gum and a card.

Grandma Evie experienced the risk of eroding purchasing power first-hand for one reason only: she invested her money exclusively in short-term fixed income instruments. Why did she do that? She was afraid of losing her money in the stock market. She wanted to protect the nominal value of her money, making sure that her $200,000 would always be $200,000. She never had to worry about opening a statement and seeing that her $200,000 had temporarily become $160,000. In 1959, her $200,000 was capable of buying goods and services costing $200,000 in 1959 prices. When she died in 2004, she left behind her $200,000 but it couldn't buy anywhere near the goods and services it could in 1959. Grandma Evie had traded the volatility of the equity market, which is temporary in nature, for a permanent loss of purchasing power.

Serious Money Investors view money as purchasing power and hence the risk of loss of money differently. Knowing that equities are the only vehicle capable of growing at a sufficient rate to keep pace with the ever-rising cost of living, and knowing that losses in the equity market are temporary, they understand that the real risk to their money is not being invested prudently in the equity market. The only skill necessary, albeit a difficult one, is being able to open a monthly statement and stomach a possible temporary decline in the account's balance.

It is incumbent upon successful investors to view risk correctly and behave accordingly. Incorrect investor behavior is protecting the nominal dollar value of your accounts by investing in fixed income instruments. Correct investor behavior is protecting the purchasing power value of your accounts by investing in equity instruments.

Fundamental Condition 3: Your Life is Complex

The world is also complex. You are continuously confronted with multi-faceted options that require complex financial decisions:

- Should I contribute to my company's 401k Plan?
- Which sub-accounts should I use?
- Do I take a full lifetime pension or the survivor option?
- How about 529 Plans for my children's educations?
- Whole life or term life insurance?

These are but a few of the questions one may face. Common sense tells you to get the help you need to make good decisions but the talking heads on TV money shows say you should be able to do this yourself. The networks have famous personalities offering financial advice to the masses, with the implication that their advice will work for everyone, including you. They strongly urge you to avoid paying anyone for something you could ostensibly do yourself. The electronic media accommodates the no-load mantra by offering all the data you could possibly want to make decisions.

With a complex world combining with the media's do-it-yourself message your ability to make correct decisions may be fogged, leaving your family vulnerable to unnecessary burdens and missed opportunities. The Serious Money Approach suggests that it may be wiser to develop a team of competent professionals to provide help along the way.

The do-it-yourself attitude may stem from a sense of rugged individualism that many of us develop as we begin our careers. We tend to do things ourselves because we cannot afford not to. This is human nature and to be expected. But rugged individualism will take us only so far in a complex world. We all need assistance from specialists and experts trained to help with the significant decisions we face as our lives become more complex.

Professionals learn how to take all the data that we encounter and transform the data into useful information. Even more importantly, experts learn how to distinguish information from wisdom. You seek wisdom, not data or information. It is the wisdom of others that will help you make better decisions.

I learned many years ago from my business coach that the problem is never the problem — the problem is that we don't know how to think about the problem. There are many ways to think about problems and you will benefit from a professional whose goal is to help you think about your problems in a complex world.

The Fog you will inevitably experience looking out the window during your long Train Ride is like the fog you sometimes encounter when you're driving on an open road. One moment you have confidence and a clear view of the road ahead, the next moment you're trapped in a bank of fog. Suddenly you lose confidence because you cannot see what's ahead. You may become confused, disoriented, stressed or worried, and you may make a poor decision.

We discussed Serious Money Principles in Chapter 2 and Serious Money Strategies in Chapter 3. When they are used in conjunction with a clear and powerful plan, the understanding that your primary risk is losing your purchasing power, and a willingness to seek the wisdom of professionals, it's like having instrument controls when you encounter the fog. Instead of making a bad decision that could result in serious long-term harm, you have a Platform of Confidence from which to approach your future, a plan to grow and protect your assets and a team to help you make better decisions about your future lifetime opportunities.

CHAPTER 5

Navigate the Western Slopes

(Understanding Bull Markets)

Board a train from Los Angeles to New York and you know you will encounter a series of western slopes you must ascend, as well as eastern slopes you must descend. It's the same when you board the Serious Money Train Ride of your financial life. Picture an historical graph of the stock market with its series of ascending and descending slopes. The ascending western slopes are the Bull Markets and the descending eastern slopes are the Bear Markets.

Each time a Bull Market ends, a Bear Market attempts to scare investors away. When enough investors have been frightened off, a Bull Market shows up to entice investors back in.

It happens every time: Bull Markets are succeeded by Bear Markets and Bear Markets are succeeded by Bull Markets. It never varies. Even when you think, "this time is different," it won't be different. Bear Markets succeed Bull Markets and Bull Markets succeed Bear Markets.

Most investors love Bull Markets and hate Bear Markets. The Serious Money Investor, however, recognizes the inevitability of the Bull Market-Bear Market cycle, understands the cycle and even embraces the Bear side of the cycle.

This chapter will explain what the Serious Money Investor knows and understands about the Bull Market part of the cycle; the following chapter will focus on the Bear Market part of the cycle.

> *"Bull Markets are born on pessimism, they grow on skepticism, they mature on optimism and they die on euphoria."* John Templeton

Born on Pessimism

All Bull Markets start from a moment at the bottom. Granted the inherent obviousness of this point, have you ever wondered why it happens that way? After all, the news is always bleak at that point, typically following a year or more of bleak news. The future always looks cloudy at best and miserable at worst. Your investments are always worth less than the year before and the country's overall wealth is less also. There are always major fiscal issues that appear unsolvable. Yet it is always within this environment of pessimism that Bull Markets begin.

This is also the very moment in time when two types of investors diverge on their path to long-term success: Serious Money Investors are invested in the market at this moment because they have faith in the future—they receive the early easy money. Other investors lost faith long ago and exited the market—they receive zero.

The beauty of the first stage of a Bull Market is that no one really knows it has started. No one, for instance, rang a bell or raised a starting flag on March 9, 2009 to announce it was time to inflect from a Bear to a Bull Market. We just began to see rising account balances on our March and April statements. Usually we see four or five statements with rising balances before the Bull earns our attention.

The best and easiest way to profit from this stage of a Bull Market is to be fully invested on Day One.

John Templeton, in the same quote above, said "You buy at the point of extreme pessimism." This is the next best way to profit because the only thing better than being fully invested at the lowest is "buying low." You may remember hearing the aphorism frequently attributed to the financier Bernard Baruch: "buy your straw hats in winter."

As easy as it may sound, it's not easy to do this. It takes courage to invest when others are frightened and think you should be too. Believing in your three Serious Money Principles is one source of such courage. It sounds like this in your head:

"Even though I don't know how to solve all these problems or even how anybody can solve these problems, and I don't know when these problems are going to be solved, I'm going to do something that has always worked; I'm going to buy low."

I once saw a picture of a dejected 5-year old sitting at the dinner table, staring at a half-eaten plate of beans and broccoli as he is about to cry. His mother has told him he can't leave the table until he eats his vegetables. The caption read: "this is what buying low feels like."

As a long-term investor, you miss out on the "pessimistic" stage of the Bull Market at your peril. The first days of this stage produce huge gains, the easy money. For example, during the first 95 days of the Bull Market that began on March 9, 2009, the Dow Jones Industrials Average rose 34%. During the subsequent 1196 days (through September 20, 2012) the same Average rose another 73% (for a total of 107%). That means investors realized approximately 1/3 of the entire gain in the first 7% of the cycle.

Over my career I've counseled hundreds of investors about proper and improper investor behavior at various points during the market cycle.

When the market is low, perhaps at its lowest point or just beyond and in the earliest stages of the next Bull Market, these are some of the behaviors that lead the Serious Money Investor to long-term success:

- <u>Your Dream House:</u> Delay purchase because the down payment money currently invested is about to grow substantially, and you would be selling it low.
- <u>Your Traditional IRA:</u> Convert to a Roth IRA because your tax bill will be its lowest and your future big gains will be tax-free.
- <u>Your Bonds:</u> Sell them to free up cash for investment in equities.
- <u>Your Mortgage:</u> Don't pay it off or accelerate principal payments because those discretionary dollars should be buying equities. Make only your minimum necessary payments.
- <u>Your New Investments:</u> Invest lump sums instead of spreading deposits over time because you're buying at what will prove to be low prices.
- <u>Your Periodic Investments:</u> Increase the size of your 401k contributions or monthly investment amounts because you can buy more shares at these low prices.
- <u>Your Current Portfolio Positions:</u> Add to them because you'll be buying low.
- <u>Your Equity Exposure:</u> Increase it because prices are low and likely going higher.

Grown on Skepticism

The next phase of the Bull Market is also noteworthy for its lack of broad acknowledgment. Savvy investors, though, know that something has changed and that there is an underlying sense of growing optimism. Most investors remain skeptical, waiting for a signal that it's okay to begin investing again because the big problems still have no sense of pending resolution.

An old adage on Wall Street says, "Bull Markets climb a wall of worry." This is the phase of the cycle where the wall of worry keeps most investors on the sidelines. The media isn't reporting solutions to the market's ills, so it feels safer to remain on the sidelines while others take the risks.

In contrast to Phase 1 of the Bull cycle, which is quite brief and usually measured in months, Phase 2 is often measured in years. Phase 2 of the 1982-2000 Bull Market lasted seven full years. During that time, the Dow Jones Industrials Average gained 109% (from December 4, 1987 to December 9, 1994).

My experience indicates that Phase 2 is marked by solid returns that match the long-term historical averages. For example, the 109% gain in the Phase 2 just described amounted to an 11% per year average annual rate of return, which is very close to the Dow's historical long-term returns. Phase 2 rates of return don't show the quick spurt out of the box of Phase 1 returns, nor do they have the spectacular returns that the later phases display.

The Serious Money Investor has been fully invested during Phases 1 and 2 and has enjoyed satisfying rates of return leading to a nice accretion of wealth. The investor who exited the previous market cycle and missed these Phases has had the satisfaction of avoiding perceived risks during pessimistic and skeptical times, but also missed an increase in account balance that is unlikely to be recaptured.

Matured on Optimism

Phase 3 is decidedly different because optimism begins to abound. Of course, Serious Money Investors have already enjoyed strong returns for a number of years, but other investors, convinced that their previous pessimism and skepticism is no longer warranted, are now ready to join the fun. They begin to feel confident that the stock market, which they had previously perceived as a money abyss, is now stable enough to produce future returns.

This newfound confidence might be attributed to any of four beliefs, three of which are false. The one belief that is likely true is that the markets are not going to retreat to the previous lows they have been awaiting. Therefore, it's now or never.

The first false belief of these investors is that having provided strong returns for a number of previous years, the market has figured out "its" problems and is now safe to enter. This belief is false for two reasons: (1) the market is never safe from temporary downturns, the type that scared the investor out in the first place; and (2) it will be increasingly difficult to achieve the long-term returns of Phases 1 and 2 because those gains were probably achieved without any significant market corrections to detract from profits.

Their second false belief is that the market has now risen to the point where they had previously exited, and so they are back to a "breakeven" point. This is a false belief because it assumes that the market magically knows, cares or remembers when they last exited the market.

Their third false belief is that some new idea has emerged and captivated the market, leading them to believe that "this time is different." This occurred in the mid-1990's when the market's problems were overridden by a growing national consensus that the dot.com companies were going to create a "new economy." No longer did conventional metrics like serious business models, sales and earnings apply; all that mattered now were "eyeballs and hits" on the internet.

But "this time is different" is a false belief because this time is never different. Sir John Templeton, the guru of investing for three decades, once said "Among the four most dangerous words in investing are 'It's different this time.'" The problems that had previously plagued investors' minds suddenly seem unimportant, even though still unresolved. This is largely a self-fulfilling belief system because solutions seem almost unnecessary: problems must not need solutions because the market is going up most days and weeks, and markets are going up because the problems must no longer be important. It's an elegant pretense while it lasts, but it's also a belief system that masks future pitfalls.

In this third phase, the market is charging ahead at full speed. Annual returns exceed historical long-term rates, meaning the ascent up the western slope is getting steeper and steeper. Investors who missed out on Phases 1 and 2 may even feel brave enough to try to catch up for missed opportunities or make extra profits over and above those being generously provided by the market.

> Big Mistake Alert! This is the time when the mistake of leverage enters the mix. *Leverage is borrowing at the wrong time to buy the wrong things for the wrong reason.* Borrowing money to invest in the market is seldom a good idea, but it is an especially poor idea during Phase 3 when optimism is high and risks of a downturn are increasing. If a downturn occurs, temporarily losing your accrued profits is one thing but temporarily losing money that wasn't yours in the first place is quite another.

What are Serious Money Investors doing during the optimistic phase? They are certainly enjoying their new profits, but they also know that the Bear Market is surely coming sooner or later. They are preparing for it by harvesting their pre-determined Target profits, and by narrowing their Target range so that Targets are reached with smaller and smaller market advances. They are also funding their Lifestyle Pool with cash to withstand the next Bear cycle with confidence.

Die on Euphoria

Eventually and inevitably, optimism mushrooms into euphoria, and the final phase of the Bull Market begins. You know you're in this phase of the market cycle when your hairdresser tells you that a stock she bought doubled almost overnight. If a dejected 5-year-old who can't leave the table until he eats his vegetables is a picture of what buying low feels like, then your hairdresser bragging about a recent stock purchase is a picture of what buying high feels like.

Alas, a sure sign that euphoria had erupted in 1998 was when an 80-year old widowed client asked me to buy Cisco Systems and Intel because she had heard about the glories of these companies on television the night before.

The surest sign that euphoria is in full swing is when annual rates of return have skyrocketed beyond all measures of sustainability. During the euphoric phase of the 1990's Bull Market, for example, the Dow Jones Industrials Average accelerated its annual rate to just over 34% per year. It should be obvious that this annual rate is not sustainable for long.

Big Mistake Alert! Buying high during this phase usually proves to be one of the biggest mistakes investors make. This is not to say that prudent purchases of companies that have not yet enjoyed a big advance is wrong. But typically, investors aren't looking for and buying these companies when they are feeling euphoric. Quite the opposite, they identify the companies that have had the biggest advances so far in the belief that they will continue to ride their waves. But buying high like this indicates a complete lack of an adult sense of danger.

I want to again emphasize that no bells are rung nor are flags raised to warn you that the Bull cycle is coming to an end soon. The approaching end of the Bull cycle also does not mean you should sell everything to avoid the likely downturn. Serious Money Investors recognize that the next part of the cycle is something to endure because it is inevitable. They have prepared for the end of the Bull part of the cycle by harvesting Target profits along the way and funding their Lifestyle Pool. And, more than anything, they don't want to exit their investments because they want to be fully invested when the next moment of maximum pessimism presents itself and the Bull cycle starts all over again.

CHAPTER 6

Navigate the Eastern Slopes

(Understanding Bear Markets)

Cross-country train rides necessarily have to navigate the eastern slopes of mountain ranges. The ride can be unsettling because of downhill speed, unprotected curves and dark tunnels. Knowing that the mountain range ends and the track eventually levels off helps mitigate the fear. The Bear Market segment of every investment cycle is similarly unnerving, and the concerns of many investors are compounded by the additional fear that there is no bottom.

Serious Money Investors view the Bear cycle differently. Many actually relish the thought of the Bear when they have money to invest and want to buy at lower prices. Others may not necessarily relish the thought but they understand and accept that Bear Markets serve an important purpose and are necessary to acquire future profits. As legendary investor Shelby

Cullom Davis explained, "You make most of your money in a Bear Market, you just don't realize it at the time."

Bear Markets are traditionally defined as a drop of 20% or more from any peak price. Their inevitability is as elementary as acknowledging that nothing goes up forever, including the prices of businesses. They must top out at some point when optimism and euphoria give way to the reality that the businesses are over-priced and can no longer be bought with the expectation of a nice future profit. When this happens, there are fewer buyers and sellers must drop their price if they want to turn their shares into cash.

Usually it doesn't take a 20% drop in price — but something less — to attract buyers back into the market. These "corrections" are an accurate description of what is taking place: market abnormalities (typically prices that are too high) correcting themselves back to more normal levels. But sometimes the market is so over-priced (typically after a multi-year Bull run) that it takes 20%, 30%, 40% or even 50%+ corrections to restore a sense of normalcy to market prices.

There have been 14 official Bear Markets since World War II, which means we average one Bear Market every 5 years or so. The average decline in price has been approximately 30% and the declines have stretched out an average of 14 months. The largest decline has been 57% (2007-09) and the longest decline has been 37 months (1946-49). In all but two of these Bear Markets, the succeeding rallies recovered 100% of the previous losses and proceeded to make new highs.

Big Mistake Alert! The biggest of the Eight Big Mistakes is Panic. It's the biggest because it is so difficult (if not impossible) to fully recover the shares lost after bailing on the market at low prices, sometimes the lowest prices, right at the moment of maximum pessimism. Panic occurs when there is a complete absence of faith in the future. I can't remember a time during my investment career when investors who bailed were rewarded in the long-term for their panic. It has always been the case that the patient, disciplined investor is the one who is rewarded long-term.

Watching the value of your investments decline by 30% is disappointing, frustrating and terrifying, all the more so if you fear that the decline will never end. But this is where Serious Money Investors have an edge because they know and believe that the Bear cycle will end…because it always does. They know it's okay to be alarmed but not okay to act out of fear. They also know that the proper strategy is to wait it out. This is the surest way to be fully invested when the Bear cycle reverses itself and becomes the next Bull cycle.

The knowledge that 14 Bear Markets since WWII have eventually ended has taught me two additional lessons. First, declines are always temporary. This lesson ties in beautifully with our second Serious Money Principle: Patience. Although we don't know (or pretend to know) when the "market problem" will end, we know that since declines are always temporary they will, in fact, end.

The second lesson, and perhaps the more important of the two, is that the primary risk of being invested in the stock market is not the risk of losing one's money, but rather the risk of not being able to stomach the inevitable downward volatility of pricing. This may seem a distinction without a difference, but it makes all the difference in the world to a Serious Money Investor. *Knowing that you won't lose your money if you can stomach the volatility gives you the courage to remain invested when all around you are scared.* This is especially true if you have a fully funded Lifestyle Pool to ensure that your cash flow won't be interrupted and that you won't have to sell your shares at low prices to meet cash needs. The Serious Money Investor can calmly watch the market do its gyrations and wait it out.

Volatility, viewed correctly, is the investor's friend, not enemy. Volatility is the mechanism by which prices fall back in line with normal values, allowing the Serious Money Investor an opportunity to buy more shares with new cash available to invest. Viewed from the perspective of one who observes our other two Principles, Faith in the Future and Discipline, a Bear Market is like a big sale, the opportunity to accumulate more shares at the lowest prices in years.

> *"A Bear Market is when investors who think this time is different sell their common stocks at panic prices to investors who think this time is never different."* Nick Murray

I'd like to reiterate a comment made earlier: it is okay to feel anxious when we are in the midst of a Bear cycle but it is not okay to act on it by selling your shares. Let's look at the two recent Bear Markets most of us lived through: the 2000-02 Bear and the 2007-09 Bear. Investors who acted on their fears in 2001 (perhaps just after September 11) when the S&P 500 Index was around 965 missed out on the subsequent rally that took the S&P to 1565, a gain of 65%. Investors who acted on their fears in 2009 when the S&P was around 825 missed out on the subsequent rally that took the S&P to 1440, a gain of 74%. The lesson here is to not get scared off the Serious Money Train because you will miss out on the rallies that always follow the end of the Bear Market cycle.

It is not necessary to accept the full brunt of a Bear cycle. There are strategies you can employ to minimize your downside volatility, and to the extent you do so, minimize the temptation to panic and get off the Train Ride. A quick lesson in the mathematics of downside volatility will serve to help you understand why lower downside volatility is a key to staying on the Train.

If your investments decline 10% in price, it takes an 11% rebound to bring you back to breakeven. If your investments decline 25%, it takes a 34% rebound to do the same. If your investments decline by 50%, it takes a 100% rebound. Clearly, the less your portfolio declines, the easier it is to get back to par.

One strategy for minimizing downside volatility is to buy low. I learned this lesson from Charles DeVaulx and Jean-Marie Eveilllard, legendary value managers who have managed mutual funds that have weathered Bear Markets better than most. Their key is to be brutally diligent about avoiding runaway prices, even when they are excited about buying a favored stock. For them, it's more than just a discipline; it's in their DNA.

I remember playing golf with Mr. DeVaulx when laser yardage devices just hit the market. Being an avid golfer, Charles was intrigued with my device and asked how much I paid for it. When I said $200, he simply shook his head and said "I'll wait to buy one when the price is under $100."

If your portfolio is largely comprised of funds managed in this way, your path to long-term success will be slow and steady, and we learned as children that slow and steady wins the race. Prove this to yourself by comparing two portfolios that each totals a 50% nominal return. Portfolio "A" is slow and steady, earning 10% annually for 5 years for a total of 50%. Portfolio "B" is aggressive, earning consecutive returns of +20%, -8%, +27%, -22% and +33%, also for a total of 50%. At the end of 5 years, the slow and steady portfolio will have increased 61%, whereas the aggressive portfolio will have increased by just 45%. It does make a difference how you achieve a 50% total return, explaining vividly why slow and steady wins the race.[2]

A third strategy for minimizing downside volatility is to include dividend-paying stocks or funds in the mix. The reason is that dividend-paying businesses tend to fall less in price during market declines because investors are willing to buy these shares sooner than non-dividend-paying shares. This is due to the mathematical certainty that as prices decline, a company's dividend yield increases, and a point is reached where investors are willing to buy shares and wait for a rebound while they are being paid an increased yield on their investment.

One final strategy for avoiding the full brunt of the Bear cycle is to be sure to harvest your pre-set profit Targets during the previous Bull cycle. If you do so, you will own fewer shares at the top of the cycle because those harvested profits are safely deposited into your Lifestyle Pool. Thus, you will have fewer shares that will take the full hit of the Bear cycle.

In summary, too many investors are scared off the Train Ride during Bear Markets because of an irrational fear that the world as they know it

---

2 Granted, I don't know of any investments that return 10% each and every year, but that isn't important. What is important is that you seek to build a portfolio that is slow and steady as possible.

is ending. Serious Money Investors don't fall prey to this thinking because they know the world has never ended and does not end. Instead, they prepare for the next Bear Market while the current market is at a relative high point. Here are some of their behaviors:

- <u>Your Dream House:</u> Buy it now because you can sell substantial profits and use the proceeds.
- <u>Your Traditional IRA:</u> Keep your Traditional IRA (don't convert it to a Roth IRA) because you'll incur maximum taxes on your gains just before the next potential drop in price.
- <u>Your Mortgage:</u> Pay it off now because you have made substantial profits and they may be about to temporarily evaporate. Alternately, use your accrued profits to accelerate your principal payments.
- <u>Your New Investments:</u> Don't invest large lump sums at high prices because you'll have an opportunity to invest at lower prices after the Bear Market ends.
- <u>Your Periodic Investments:</u> Continue to contribute to your 401k plan or other monthly investment programs because your periodic deposits will buy more shares as prices fall.
- <u>Your Equity Exposure:</u> Decrease it because prices are high and perhaps headed lower.

CHAPTER 7

The Wheels Are Screeching

(Distinguishing Noise from Wisdom)

The strange noises you hear when traveling can make you uncomfortable, like the first time you heard the jarring howl of an airplane lowering its landing gear. As you traveled more, noises became normalized and you learned to distinguish between normal and truly abnormal noise, growing wiser in the process.

Being an investor is a similar experience. Investment noise is continuous and ubiquitous, and until that noise becomes normalized it's likely to threaten and cause bad investor behavior at the most inopportune times.

Investment noise takes many forms. It might be an ominous economic prediction from the news media, financial pundits speculating on matters of no long-term significance, the latest doomsday book to hit the press or hearsay from your brother-in-law at Thanksgiving dinner. The Serious Money Investor learns to tune out these noises and focus instead on the big picture themes that supersede the daily noise. These are the pearls of wisdom that have survived the years.

I have been fortunate during my career to meet and learn from great thinkers who have allowed me to accumulate and integrate these pearls into my own thinking. I believe in these pearls and I suggest you embrace them also. They will serve you well when you are assaulted by daily noise, know you should reject it, but need something more powerful to replace it.

Role of News

Years ago, when there were no cable news stations, Nick Murray taught me that the business of news is to sell news even when there is no news. This pearl is all the more relevant given today's 24/7 news immersion on television and the internet. The news never provides a long-term perspective on today's issues. Making my point, if television's business shows advised us to focus on our 25-year game plans instead of what's happening at the moment, we would all stop watching. Obviously, I am not suggesting that being current with the news isn't important. But relying on the news to help you formulate big picture goals and strategies isn't something that the Serious Money Investor does.

Optimism is Realism

Perhaps being generally optimistic is a necessary trait for a good investment advisor since it is difficult to recommend investing in the future if one doesn't believe the future is going to be worth investing in. But I have tried to pass along my overall sense of optimism to our Serious Money Investor clients, not simply because I am optimistic but because I believe it is realistic to be optimistic.

Suggesting this notion to me years ago, Nick Murray explained how difficult it is to reconcile a cynical, skeptical perspective with the harsh realities of the 20th century. During that 100-year period, we witnessed the mainstreaming of electricity and the automobile, we liberated millions of people from dictatorships, we legislated civil rights for all Americans and we invented new technologies that allowed us to land on the moon. We also survived the threat of nuclear destruction, ended the Cold War and led the world toward modernization. No doubt you can think of many other incredible achievements.

Despite all the problems we faced and solved, not to mention all the problems we faced and didn't solve, our standard of living increased multi-fold to where even our poorest live better than royalty of times past. How can one not view humanity's awesome progress through an optimistic lens? I have concluded that being cynical and skeptical is not the correct way to perceive the human condition. Just the opposite: to me, optimism is realism.

Is it different this time? Are our current problems so menacing and unique that it's unrealistic to be optimistic about the future? You already know the answer to the first question: no, this time isn't different. The answer to the second question is also no; it is entirely realistic to be optimistic about our future. There are many reasons to be optimistic that are beyond the scope of this book (but please consider reading *Abundance*, by Peter Diamandis, for a full treatment of the subject). Two reasons are within its scope, however: microchips and entrepreneurs.

The Microchip Trend

No trend is bigger than the microchip trend. It is already embedded in most activities of daily living and its presence will only continue to grow in our lives. I know you are well aware of the amazing advances the microchip has brought to your personal and work life in the last 20 years. It's almost unimaginable that 20 years ago we didn't have the internet, email, text and instant messaging, search or social networking capabilities.

It was just 30 years ago that we acquired rudimentary spreadsheet and word processing capabilities.

Over the past quarter century, everyone has acquired (1) the potential capability to access virtually any and all known information, (2) the potential capability to communicate with anyone in the world, and (3) the capability to join communities that share common interests anywhere in the world. This is powerful stuff because it essentially means that human beings have the capability to reorganize the planet digitally. No longer must we organize ourselves by family, religion, social or financial status, or even by country. We can still choose to do so, but we now have the freedom to organize person-to-person as well as person-to-community-of-interest.

The microchip hits bureaucracies especially hard. Dan Sullivan is fond of saying "the microchip eats bureaucracies for lunch." This applies to all bureaucracies, whether they are organized for business, non-profit or government. The power of the microchip — more accurately the power of individuals who use the microchip — to effect change far exceeds the ability of a bureaucracy to keep pace.

We have already seen instances where the microchip has decimated non-digital bureaucratic business models: think back to the newspaper model of 10 years ago, supported primarily by classified advertising. When Craig's List came online, classified advertising was doomed, and so was the newspaper business model. The video store business model had a respite from the microchip as we converted from tape to DVDs, but finally succumbed as we converted from DVD to downloading. As you think about your daily activities that have already replaced activities from years past, you begin to sense the power of the microchip trend.

The microchip is also changing the nature of government policy-making, which is becoming less powerful than the organizing activities of individuals and smaller groups, both for good and bad ends. Al Qaeda has been successful because of its digital network, and the Arab Spring of 2011 in Egypt was also organized digitally. The Tea Party movement of 2009-10 organized hundreds of like-minded groups digitally and became so powerful in the short span of 18 months it helped shift control of the House of Representatives from Democrat to Republican.

I believe that the source of most of our country's financial ills is the government, our biggest bureaucracy. Until recently, individuals had little ability to impact laws, policies and regulations. That has changed with cheap access to the microchip, which has become one of the Serious Money Investor's best friends because of its ability to effect, change or even topple bad government policy. We can now change course if enough persons become motivated to do so.

Bad government policy is no match for the triumvirate power of the microchip, an idea whose time has come and a network of motivated persons. This alone is reason enough for The Serious Money Investor to remain optimistic about the future.

By the way, in the ongoing battle between the microchip and bureaucracy, make no mistake which will get stronger faster. Gordon Moore, of Intel fame, many years ago stated what has become known as Moore's Law: every 18 months, the power of the microchip doubles while its cost halves. This means that before you are two years older than you are today, individuals who use microchips will have twice the capability they have now. Do you know of any bureaucracy that can say the same thing?

The Role of Entrepreneurs

The primary beneficiary of the microchip trend is the entrepreneur, and the role of the entrepreneur is cause for additional optimism. The entrepreneur has been the primary job creator in this country for several decades. The role of the entrepreneur is to identify resources not being fully or adequately utilized, and bring those resources to a higher and better utilization. This is what the small businessperson does. This is the value that the small businessperson brings.

More often than not, today's entrepreneur finds that the cracks that need filling are in the walls of bureaucracies (again, think about Craig's

List and the role it played in the downfall of the newspaper model). Entrepreneurism fills a longing in the American spirit. If entrepreneurs have become the major employment vehicle in the country, their numbers will only multiply in the near term as many of our country's recently-unemployed will permanently abandon working for major bureaucratic employers. They will fulfill long-held dreams of starting their own businesses, partnering with their buddies, inventing new stuff, raising our standards of living and making more money than they could have earned being an employee of a bureaucratic entity.

Of course, many will fail, and many of those who fail the first time will get it right the next time. This is in keeping with the American Way.

Less and less do governments control our path of future progress. More and more it is instead in the hands of the entrepreneur armed with power of the microchip and connected to communities of interest via social networks.

This is something about which to be optimistic.

CHAPTER 8

Is This Your Stop?

(Buy a Companion Ticket)

Rugged individualism is typically thought to be a positive personality trait because it instigates much of our progress. It's required to start a new business, pursue higher education or advance a career. While a certain level of success can be attained through rugged individualism, rarely do we consider its flip side: the personal ceiling it can create. Successful individuals soon realize the limits that arise when one is going it alone.

Once that success ceiling is reached, rugged individualists discover they must manage more than the unique activities that gave rise to the initial venture. They also are now responsible for all the other activities of the enterprise: those at which they may excel but also those at which they are merely competent or even inept.

The only way to break through the ceiling is to delegate these activities. There are other individuals for whom these activities are unique. Your goal should be to build a unique team with these individuals, allowing you to focus on your own unique activities and abilities.

Delegating to others and building your unique team cost money, of course, but your success will multiply as you delegate. You will make more than enough money to pay for your delegations and have excess money left over, along with achievements that were unattainable otherwise. Dan Sullivan explains, "There is nothing you can't achieve if you are willing to ask for and pay for the help of others."

Your sense of rugged individualism can play a role in the ultimate success you experience on the Serious Money Train Ride of your life. Ask yourself whether it is your unique ability to develop a coherent financial plan or roadmap, identify the investment vehicles and strategies that will take you down the correct path of your plan, and most importantly, stay on track despite all of the different noises that will try to throw you off track. If these are not your unique abilities, you should consider delegating them by adding a financial advisor as a key member of your unique team.

Each time you hear investment noise during your trip, our metaphorical conductor will knock on your compartment door and ask, "Is this your stop? Do you want to get off the Train here?" You'll need to make the right decision every time while all this noise is going on around you. You'll soon learn that the real work of the Train Ride of your life is trying to distinguish the investment noise from important investment information and wisdom. Do not make the mistake of thinking that it is easy to make these distinctions or that it gets easier over time. In fact, the process gets incrementally harder because investment noise attempts to disguise itself so that you think the noise is actually important investment information. The hidden agenda of investment noise is to have you incorrectly answer the conductor's query with, "yes, I think this is my stop and I'd like to get off now, please."

The good news is that the investment industry has built two different kinds of compartments on this Train: one for the rugged individualists and one for the delegators. The first compartment is called the Family Compartment, and there are just enough seats for you and your family to take your Train Ride together. It is priced inexpensively. If you hope to get where you're going inexpensively or on your own, this is your compartment. There are many good investment choices that are inexpensive, and the money you save by doing it yourself will come in handy down the road if you don't like where you end up or you find that you have to do it all over again with help.

On the other hand, if you want to carefully and realistically identify a specific future destination and you want a professional to take responsibility for helping ensure that you actually get there, you should ride in the Professional Compartment. This compartment has enough seats for you and your family but it also holds one additional seat for someone like me, a financial professional. It's a more expensive compartment, but the price is reasonable. You will be able to focus on what you do best while the professional sits beside you and coaches you during your trip.

Of course, paying for a professional's seat beside you doesn't mean anything is guaranteed since this is art, not science. But when we encounter some investment noise and the conductor knocks on the door to ask whether this is your stop and whether you'll be getting off the train here, the professional will be there to help you make the right decision. Together, we'll be able to evaluate whether it's just investment noise we're hearing or whether it's important investment information that we should consider.

Big Mistake Alert! We've now covered seven of Eight Big Mistakes, but there is one final Big Mistake to which you should be alert: Cost. This mistake occurs when you allow cost to become an emotional influence in your decision-making. For example, you might allow what you paid for an investment to emotionally influence whether you sell or hang on to it. Perhaps you will allow the tax cost of selling a profitable investment to emotionally influence your decision, or permit the cost of a seat in the Train's Professional Compartment to emotionally influence your decision to ask for help from a qualified professional.

Cost should not emotionally influence these decisions. The determining factor should be the value received. I believe that riding in the Professional Compartment, hiring someone like me to sit next to you and your family during this ride, provides a value that makes it much more likely you will arrive comfortably at your destination.

Summary

What we've covered in this book is a comprehensive and strategic approach to managing your Serious Money. I've found it useful to think of this approach as a lifelong cross-country train ride because graphically your journey should resemble the upwardly sloping path from Los Angeles to New York.

Your successful investment journey requires a Platform of Confidence because this train ride will encounter many scary dips, curves, and tunnels that will test your mettle all along the way. We discussed three Ground Rules for developing your confidence:

- It's okay to refresh your starting point no matter what's worked and what hasn't to this point in your life.
- Don't wait for a better time to invest because the best time to invest is when you have the money.
- Take advantage of big sales just like you do whenever your favorite stores are offering discount prices.

The Train Ride comes with a manifesto of three Serious Money Principles to guide you and provide a source of strength and conviction that you will need to complete your journey:

- Have faith in the future of human progress because this will provide not only the reason for investing in the first place but also the context for interpreting crisis stories and the firewall you need to avoid making one of the Eight Big Mistakes. It's okay to not know how any of the big problems will be resolved.

- Have patience because it's also okay to not know when these big problems will be resolved.
- Have the discipline to engage in investment behaviors that have stood the test of time and avoid investment behaviors that are new and different.

We explained three important investment Strategies designed to help you implement our Principles:

- The first strategy divides your money into two pools: a Lifestyle Pool and a Profit-making pool, with each pool serving a distinctly different purpose.
- The second strategy spreads your money so all of your eggs aren't in one basket.
- The third strategy protects your profits by taking advantage of higher prices.

You will be tested repeatedly along your journey to see if you have the fortitude to remain on the Ride. The tests are unending and inevitable because we live in a world that is busy, risky and complex with a media that consistently suggests solutions that steer you in the wrong direction. The Serious Money approach instead offers these recommendations to help you stay on track:

- Make a plan and review it often.
- Understand that your real risk is the long-term loss of your purchasing power.
- Understand that accessing data and information is not enough—it is the wisdom of professionals that you should seek.

Any cross-country investment journey will entail ascending the western slopes known as Bull Markets. Most Bull Markets unfold in four phases which have distinct features that need to be understood to take full advantage:

- The pessimistic phase is the first phase, wherein maximum early gains can be realized.
- The skeptical phase is next, wherein the market typically climbs a wall of worry.
- The optimistic phase is fun but also suggests it's time to prepare for corrections and next Bear Market.
- The finale is the euphoric phase, which is exhilarating but requires prudence and understanding of what comes next.

What comes next is a Bear Market, the predictable and necessary descent down the eastern slopes. Although some investors will try to avoid this descent, the Serious Money investor understands the role of Bear Markets and their importance to your long-term success. Our approach offers several strategies for mitigating the havoc that Bear Markets can wreak:

- Recognize that Bear Markets end, even if you think that this time will be different.
- Use mutual fund managers whose discipline is to always buy low because the mathematics of downside volatility will be in your favor.
- Incorporate dividend-paying stocks in your portfolio because they tend to rebound sooner during down markets.
- Be sure to have harvested profits during previous Bull Market so that you own fewer shares that decline during the Bear Market.

Throughout your long investment journey you will hear investment noise. It will take many forms, it will be continuous, and you must learn to normalize and reject it, and replace it with powerful pearls of wisdom:

- The business of news is to sell news even when there is no news.
- Optimism has been realism, and this time is not different.

- The most powerful trend, bar none, is the absorption of the microchip into our daily lives, giving individuals the capability to access information, communicate with anyone, and join communities of interest. Don't bet against this trend.
- The primary beneficiary of the microchip trend is the entrepreneur, who is now capable of dismantling old business models and providing alternatives to over-bearing government policies and regulations.

Finally, continuing our train ride metaphor, know that you will be asked a question by the conductor of this train every time you hear investment noise. The question will sound something like, "Do you want to get off the Train here?" You will need to make the correct call each time.

An important decision you will need to make, recognizing that a certain level of success can be attained through your own sense of rugged individualism, is whether you want to go it alone or buy a companion seat for a trusted professional to sit beside you. Although buying a companion ticket does not guarantee your success, your trusted professional can help you make the right call and avoid the Eight Big Mistakes we discussed throughout the book.

It is my hope that the journey that is the one and only financial Train Ride of your life be filled with confidence, peace of mind and more success than you ever dreamed imaginable.